Oh CHEESE!
Homestyle Cheesy Favorites

by Lora C. Mercado

Marguerite Publishing
www.margueritepublishing.com

CONTENTS

Introduction

Cheese is one of the most comforting ingredients you can add to a recipe. There are so many wonderful types to choose from, each with it's own unique flavor.

In this book, I have put together a selection of my all time favorite homestyle cheesy dishes. Feel free to substitute the type of cheese in the recipe with one of your favorites. Add extra if you like!

You will find that these recipes are simple to follow, quick to make and taste delightful. You can never go wrong with cheese!

Enjoy!

~ Lora Mercado

Amazing Artichoke Dip

1 can artichoke hearts (chopped)
1 small can green chillies(chopped)
1/2 cup Parmesan cheese
3/4 cup mayonnaise
1 - 8oz package shredded cheddar cheese
Garlic powder to taste

Combine chopped artichoke hearts with all the ingredients except the shredded cheese. Pour into a 9" pie plate and top with cheese. Bake for 20 minutes at 350 degrees. Serve with crackers.

Bacon and Cheese Potatoes

2 lbs small red potatoes (quartered)
1/2 cup ranch dressing
1/2 cup shredded cheddar cheese
1/4 cup bacon bits
1 TB parsley

Combine dressing, cheese and bacon bits in a large bowl. Add potatoes to mixture and coat thoroughly. Place in a greased 9x13" pan and cover with foil. Bake for 40 minutes at 350 degrees. Remove foil and cook an additional 15 minutes or until potatoes are done. Sprinkle with parsley before serving.

Bacon Chicken Rolls

6 skinless boneless chicken breasts
6 slices of bacon
1 T butter
8 oz whipped cream cheese with chives

Pound out chicken breasts between two pieces of waxed paper until about 1/2" thick. Spread 3 tablespoons of cream cheese mixture onto each piece of chicken. Add 1/2 tsp butter. Fold ends of chicken over filling. Wrap a slice of bacon around each rolled chicken breast. Place in baking dish, seam down. Bake for 40 minutes at 400 degrees or until chicken is tender and no longer pink. Broil for five minutes or until bacon is crispy.

Bacon and Swiss Pie

12 sliced bacon (cooked crisp and crumbled)
1 cup shredded Swiss cheese
1/3 cup onion (chopped)
1/8 tsp black pepper
2 cups milk
1 cup Bisquick baking mix
4 eggs
1/4 tsp salt

Grease a 10" pie plate. Place bacon, cheese and onion in the plate. In a medium bowl, beat the remaining ingredients until a smooth consistency with a hand mixer. Pour over bacon mixture. Bake for 35-40 minutes at 400 degrees, or until a knife inserted in the middle comes out clean. Let cool for 5 minutes before serving.

Broccoli Cheese Chicken Pot Pie

10 oz package frozen broccoli (cooked)
1 - 8 oz can water chestnuts (drained and chopped)
1/4 cup butter
1/4 cup flour
1 tsp salt
1/2 tsp paprika
2 1/4 cups milk
1/2 cup shredded cheddar cheese
1 can sliced mushrooms (drained)
2 cups cooked chicken (chopped)
Prepared pie crust
1 egg yolk
2 TB water

In a skillet, over low heat, melt butter. Stir in flour, salt and paprika. Gradually add milk, and cook on low, stirring until mixture becomes thick and smooth. Slowly add broccoli, water chestnuts, mushrooms, chicken and cheese. Place in 2 1/2 quart casserole dish. Cover top with pie crust, and seal edges. Combine egg yolk and water. Cut slits in top of crust, then brush with egg yolk and water mixture. Bake for 40 minutes at 375 degrees.

Bruschetta Chicken Bake

3-4 boneless, skinless chicken breasts (cubed)
1 can diced tomatoes
1 package chicken flavored stuffing mix
2 cloves garlic (minced)
1 tsp oregano
1 cup shredded mozzarella cheese

Combine undrained can of tomatoes, garlic, stuffing mix and 1/2 cup water. Mix until stuffing is well moistened, set aside. Place chicken in 9x13" pan and sprinkle with oregano and cheese. Top with stuffing mixture. Bake for 30 minutes in a 400 degree oven, until chicken is no longer pink.

Cheddar Cheese Dollars

1/2 lb shredded sharp cheddar cheese
1/2 cup butter (softened)
1 cup flour
1/2 tsp salt

Combine above ingredients, mix well. Roll into a log shape and wrap in waxed paper. Refrigerate for 2 hours. Slice into 1/4" slices and sprinkle with Parmesan cheese and paprika. Bake for 8 minutes in a 500 degree oven. Keep an eye on these, so they do not burn. Cool on wire rack. Serve warm or at room temperature.

Cheddar Cheese Soup

1 cup celery (chopped)
2 carrots (chopped or grated)
1 small onion (chopped)
1/2 tsp dry mustard
1/2 tsp black pepper
2 cups beef bouillon
1/4 cup butter
2 TB flour
1 tsp salt
2 cups milk
2 cups shredded sharp cheddar cheese

Saute onions, carrots and celery in butter until soft. Mix in flour, salt, mustard. Add bouillon. Cook on medium heat, stirring constantly until thickened. Add milk and heat to boiling. Reduce heat and simmer on low for ten minutes. Add shredded cheese immediately before serving.

Cheddar Zucchini Bake

6 cups zucchini (thinly sliced)
2 TB butter
1/8 tsp black pepper
1 tsp salt
Garlic powder to taste
1 - 8oz can tomato sauce
1 1/2 cup shredded sharp cheddar cheese

Melt butter in a skillet, add zucchini, pepper, salt, garlic powder, and tomato sauce. Mix well, then add half of the cheese, stirring until melted. Pour into greased 1 1/2 quart casserole dish. Top with remaining cheese and bake for 20 minutes at 375 degrees.

Cheese Ball

2 - 8oz packages cream cheese
2 TB onion (chopped)
1 TB pimento (chopped)
1/4 cup green pepper (chopped)
2 cups pecans or walnuts (chopped)
1 tsp seasoned salt
8.5oz crushed pineapple

Combine all ingredients and form into a large ball. Roll in additional chopped nuts if desired. Chill in refrigerator and serve with crackers.

Cheesy Beefy Rotini

6 oz rotini noodles (cooked and drained)
1 lb ground beef
Salt, pepper and garlic powder to taste
1 - 14 oz can stewed tomatoes
1 cup green onions (chopped)
1 - 3 oz package cream cheese
1/2 cup shredded sharp cheddar cheese
1/2 cup shredded Swiss cheese
1/2 cup shredded Parmesan cheese

Brown ground beef in skillet and add seasonings to taste. Drain. Add stewed tomatoes, then simmer uncovered, on low until it starts to thicken. Stir in cream cheese and green onions. Add cooked pasta. Mix in three kinds of cheese, and cover until melted.

Cheesy Lunch Pockets

2 oz cream cheese (softened)
1 TB Miracle Whip
1 tsp Dijon mustard
4 slices of deli ham, chicken or turkey (chopped)
1/4 cup shredded mozzarella cheese
1 can refrigerated biscuits

Combine cream cheese, Miracle Whip and mustard. Add deli meat and cheese. Mix until well blended. Set aside. Flatten each biscuit into a 3 1/2" circle. Place a heaping teaspoon of the cream cheese mixture in the center of each dough circle. Fold dough in half and seal edges by pressing together. Bake 10-12 minutes in a 400 degree oven, until lightly browned.

Cheesy Vegetable Quiche

16 oz California mix frozen vegetables
1/2 cup onion (chopped)
1/2 cup green pepper (chopped)
2 T olive oil or butter
1 cup shredded cheddar cheese
1 cup shredded Swiss cheese
2 T flour
2 pie shells
8 eggs
1 large can evaporated milk
1 tsp salt
1/4 tsp pepper

In a skillet, saute' onions and green pepper in olive oil or butter until soft. In a bowl, beat together eggs, milk, salt and pepper. Place pie shells in pie pans. Evenly divide the ingredients into both pies. Layer cheese on the bottom, then add onions and green pepper, then vegetables. Sprinkle flour over top and mix gently. Pour egg mixture over the top of each pie. Bake for 35-40 minutes at 400 degrees. Quiche is done when knife inserted comes out clean. Let set for 10 minutes prior to serving.

Chili Cheese Rice

1 cup white rice
2 cups chicken broth
1 TB chili powder
1/2 cup sour cream
1 cup shredded Monterey Jack cheese
Hot Sauce to taste

In a medium saucepan, combine rice, broth and chili powder. Bring to a boil for one minute. Reduce heat to low and simmer covered for 20 minutes. After simmered, remove from heat and let cool for five minutes. Fold in sour cream, cheese and hot sauce. Pour into greased 9x13" casserole dish. Bake 15-20 minutes in a 350 degree oven, until lightly browned.

Cream Cheese Chicken Puffs

3 oz Cream cheese
2 T butter
2 T milk
1/4 tsp salt
1/8 tsp black pepper
1 T onion (chopped)
2 cups cooked chicken (chopped)
1 package crescent rolls

Combine all the above ingredients together, except for the crescent rolls. Shape each crescent roll into a rectangle. Drop 1/4 cup of the mixture onto each piece of dough. Fold over and press edges to seal closed. Place on a greased baking sheet and cook for 20-25 minutes at 350 degrees.

Easy Enchiladas

1 can cream of chicken soup
1 can chopped green chilies
1 carton sour cream
1 bunch green onions (finely chopped)
1 dozen tortillas
1 lb shredded sharp cheddar cheese

Combine soup, chilies, sour cream and onions, and simmer on low heat. Warm tortillas until soft. In each tortilla, place sauce, then roll and put into a casserole dish. Cover with shredded cheese. Bake for 20 minutes in a 350 degree oven.

Eggplant Parmesan

2 - 8 oz cans tomato sauce
2 medium eggplants (peeled and sliced)
1/2 cup grated Parmesan cheese
1-2 lbs sliced Mozzarella cheese
4- 5 eggs
2-4T olive oil

Saute' sliced eggplant in olive oil for two minutes each side. Beat eggs in separate bowl. Layer eggplant, sauce, eggs, Parmesan, then mozzarella. Repeat. End with mozzarella. Bake for 20 minutes at 350 degrees.

Ham and Cheese Bake

1 package crescent rolls
2 cups cooked ham (cubed)
1 TB Parmesan cheese
2 T green pepper (chopped)
8 oz Monterey Jack cheese (cut into 1/2" cubes)
2 eggs
Salt and pepper to taste

Lay crescent rolls on the bottom of a pie plate to form a crust layer. In a bowl, beat eggs, Parmesan cheese and salt and pepper. Mix in ham, cheese and green pepper. Pour on top of crust. With remaining crescent rolls, lay out a lattice strip pattern on top of pie. Bake for 45 minutes in a 350 degree oven, until golden brown.

Hearty Chicken Casserole

3-4 boneless, skinless chicken breasts (cooked and cubed)
1 can cream of chicken soup
1 can green beans (drained)
1 can sliced mushrooms (drained)
1 cup shredded cheddar cheese
1/2 cup mayonnaise
1 tsp lemon juice
1-10 oz pkg biscuits
2 T butter (melted)
1/2 cup crushed corn flakes

Combine chicken, soup, beans, mushrooms, cheese, mayonnaise and juice in a saucepan and heat until boiling. Pour into greased 2 quart casserole dish. Arrange biscuits in one layer over top of chicken mixture. Brush biscuits with melted butter and top with crushed corn flakes. Bake uncovered for 25-30 minutes at 375 degrees.

Homestyle Mac and Cheese

2 cups elbow macaroni (cooked)
2 cups shredded sharp cheddar cheese
2 cups milk
1 egg
1 small onion (chopped)
Salt and pepper to taste

In a small bowl, beat together milk and egg. In greased casserole dish, layer noodles, milk and egg mixture, onion and cheese. End with cheese and sprinkle top with salt and pepper. Bake for 35-45 minutes until lightly browned on top in a 350 degree oven.

Mexican Fudge

2 cups shredded cheddar cheese
2 cups shredded Monterey Jack cheese
1/2 cup green enchilada sauce
1/2 cup green taco sauce
3 eggs

In a small bowl combine enchilada sauce, taco sauce and eggs until thoroughly mixed. In a medium bowl combine both cheeses until well blended. In a 9x9" baking pan, place half of the cheese mix on the bottom. Pour taco sauce mixture over cheese, then top with remaining cheese. Bake for 30 minutes in a 350 degree oven. Cut into one inch squares and serve with tortilla chips. Tastes best served warm.

Mushroom Cheese Strata

4 eggs (beaten)
1 - 13 oz can chicken broth
1/2 cup sour cream
2 tsp Dijon mustard
8 slices white bread (cut into cubes)
1 cup shredded cheddar cheese
1 cup shredded Swiss cheese
1 can sliced mushrooms (drained)

Combine beaten eggs, chicken broth, sour cream and mustard in a large bowl. Fold in bread cubes, mushrooms and cheese. Pour into greased 2 quart casserole dish or 9x13" baking dish. Cover and refrigerate overnight.
Bake uncovered for 50-60 minutes in a 350 degree oven. Let stand 5-10 minutes before serving.

Pierogi Casserole

3 cups prepared mashed potatoes (instant or homemade)
1/2 stick butter
1 lb shredded cheddar cheese
2 onions (diced)
6 lasagna noodles (cooked)

Grease a 9x13" pan. In a skillet, saute' onions in butter. Combine cooked onions with cooked mashed potatoes. Lay three cooked noodles in the bottom of the pan. Next add a thin layer of potatoes, then cheese. Repeat the noodles, potato and cheese layer. Cover with foil. Bake for 25-30 minutes at 350 degrees.

Pineapple Cheese Casserole

2 large cans chunk pineapple (drained, save the juice)
2 cups shredded sharp cheddar cheese
4 TB flour
1 1/2 cups sugar

Topping:
1 sleeve Ritz crackers (crushed)
1 stick butter (melted)

Combine 6 tablespoons of the drained pineapple juice, cheese and flour. Add pineapple. Pour into 9x13" baking dish. Combine crackers and butter and pour on top of pineapple mixture. Bake for 30 minutes at 350 degrees.

Rice Delight

1/2 cup cream cheese with chives (softened)
1 egg (beaten)
2 cups cooked instant rice
1 - 15 oz can Mexicorn
1 cup sharp cheddar cheese
Dash of onion powder
Dash of black pepper

Blend cream cheese and egg until well mixed. Stir in rice, corn, 3/4 cup of cheese and seasonings. Pour into a greased 1 1/2 quart baking dish and top with remaining cheese. Bake for 20-25 minutes in a 375 degree oven.

Sausage and Cheese Puffs

1 lb Italian sausage (mild or hot)
2 cups shredded sharp cheddar cheese
3 cups Bisquick baking mix
3/4 cups water

Remove sausage casing and brown in a skillet until no longer pink. Drain. When sausage is cooled, combine with remaining ingredients. Roll into one inch balls and place on cookie sheet two inches apart. Bake at 400 degrees until golden brown.

Shepherd's Pie

1 lb lean ground beef
1 small onion (chopped)
2 cups freshly made mashed potatoes
4 oz package cream cheese (cubed)
1 cup sharp cheddar cheese
2 cloves garlic (minced)
4 cups frozen mixed vegetables (thawed)
1 cup beef gravy

Brown ground beef and onions until cooked through. Drain grease. Combine potatoes, cream cheese, garlic and 1/2 cup shredded cheese, until mixed well. Stir gravy and vegetables into meat, then pour into a 9x9" baking dish. Add potato mixture on top of meat mixture. Sprinkle with remaining cheese. Bake for 20 minutes in a 375 degree oven, until lightly browned.

Spinach Balls Appetizer

2 - 10 oz packages frozen spinach
3 1/2 cups onion and sage stuffing mix
1 cup Parmesan cheese
6 eggs (beaten)
3/4 cup bitter (softened)

Combine all ingredients except for the spinach. Warm spinach in pan until just thawed, remove excess liquid in spinach, then mix with other ingredients.Form into balls and place onto a greased cookie sheet. Bake for 10 minutes at 350 degrees.

Squash Heaven

2 lbs yellow squash (chopped)
2 eggs (beaten)
2 TB sugar
1 small onion (chopped)
Dash of black pepper
1 - 15oz can evaporated milk
1/4 lb shredded cheddar cheese
1 tsp salt
3/4 cup crushed potato chips
2 Tb butter (melted)

Steam squash and onions in a large pot until soft. Place in a large bowl. Add evaporated milk,salt, pepper, butter, eggs, sugar and shredded cheese. Combine until well mixed. Pour into a greased 8x10" baking dish. Top with crushed potato chips. Bake for 45 minutes in a 325 degree oven.

Stuffed Mushrooms

40 mushrooms
3/4 cup Parmesan cheese
1- 8 oz package cream cheese (softened)
2-4TB milk
Slivered almonds

Remove stems from each mushroom. Beat together cream cheese, Parmesan and milk. Pour in milk slowly, only using enough to make to make a thick, pasty consistency. Fill mushrooms with mixture, and place a slivered almond on top of each one. Broil 3-5 minutes.

Swiss Vegetable Casserole

2 large bags of vegetable medley (broccoli, cauliflower, carrots)
2 cans water chestnuts
1 cup Swiss cheese
1/3 cup sour cream
1/4 tsp black pepper
1 can cheddar cheese soup
1 can French fried onions

Mix vegetables, 1/2 cup shredded cheese, soup, pepper, sour cream and half the can of fried onions. Pour into a casserole dish. Bake uncovered for 40 minutes at 350 degrees.
Top with remaining onion and cheese. Bake uncovered for an additional five minutes until lightly browned.

Taco Pie

1 pound lean ground beef
1 package taco seasoning
1 can refried beans
1/3 cup mild taco sauce
1 medium onion (chopped)
1 cup shredded sharp cheddar cheese
1 cup corn chips (crushed)
1 package crescent rolls or pie crust

Line a pie plate with crescent rolls or pie crust dough. Bake for 10 minutes at 400 degrees. Brown ground beef and onion, drain. Add taco seasoning. In separate bowl combine beans and taco sauce.
In crust, layer 1/2 bean mixture, 1/2 meat, 1/2 cheese, and all of the corn chips. Repeat layers ending with cheese on top. Bake for 20-25 minutes at 350 degrees. Top with shredded lettuce and chopped tomatoes. Serve with sour cream.

NOTES:

Be sure to check out these other titles by

Lora C Mercado:

Tasteful Memories, A Collection of Family Comfort Food
Recipes
http://www.amazon.com/dp/B00IPMF64K

Gimme That Chocolate! A PMS Survival Cookbook
http://www.amazon.com/dp/B00IT63L8U

Our Angels Await, Stories of Love from Beyond
http://www.amazon.com/dp/B00FIV93OA

Uniting Hearts, A Guide to Becoming a Wedding Officiant
http://www.amazon.com/dp/B00FXFY2MY

Departed, A Collection of Historical Cemetery Photography
http://www.amazon.com/dp/B00GEE2CRA